SUCCESSFUL COOKING

STIR-FRY

INDEX

Contents

The art of stir-frying

Once the ingredients are prepared, the secret of stir-frying is to cook quickly over high heat and keep the food moving constantly around the wok.

Stir-frying is a fast, relatively healthy way to cook food. It involves quick cooking where the food is tossed around in a wok over high heat in a minimum amount of oil. Preparation of ingredients is essential because once you start to cook there is no time to chop anything extra or hunt through the cupboard for an extra bottle of sauce.

OILS

Use oils for stir-frying that have a high smoking point. These include canola oil and peanut oil. Olive oil may be used to add flavour to warm stir-fry salads. If you are trying to cut down on fat, use an oil spray.

INGREDIENTS

Seafood: Quick cooking suits seafood perfectly. Squid, prawns and scallops need the briefest possible time in the wok until they are cooked through. Use firm-fleshed fish so it can be stir-fried without breaking up.

Meat and Poultry: Meat to be stir-fried needs to be from a cut which will be tender after only a short cooking time. It should be cut across the grain into strips or small pieces so it cooks quickly. Use chicken breast or thigh. Marinating meat or chicken helps to tenderise it and allows flavours to permeate the meat. Make sure the marinade is drained well before stir-frying, otherwise the meat or chicken will tend to steam rather than fry.

Vegetables: Stir-frying affects different vegetables in different ways. The intense heat caramelizes their sugar, but retains most of their vitamins and colour. Vegetables such as cauliflower, potatoes and carrots require a slightly longer cooking time and should be cut into small pieces or thin strips, whereas peas, asparagus and mushrooms should be cooked quickly at the end. Bean sprouts, herbs and greens, such as bok choy and spinach, should be added for the final minute or so, but for no longer because they will wilt quickly.

WOKS

There are many different types of woks available. The traditional basic wok is made of carbon steel. In its modern form the wok comes made of copper, stainless steel, cast iron and non-stick materials. Buy the heaviest wok you can find as it will retain heat well without scorching. You can also buy electric woks, which we have used in this book for our step-by-step photographs. These are non-stick and are kept at a constant high heat by an electric element.

The shape of a wok should be wide with deep, sloping sides and a round or wide, flattish bottom. It should be about 30–35 cm (12–14 inches) in diameter as small amounts of food can be cooked easily enough in a large wok but not vice versa. Flat-bottomed woks work well on electric stovetops as they sit directly on the hotplate – a wok ring

often holds the wok too far away from the heat source to get it sufficiently hot for stir-frying. Some of the more modern stovetops have a special wide gas burner for woks.

Wok lids are important as they can be used to form a seal for a couple of minutes to steam any slower cooking ingredients or greens.

If you do not have a wok, you can use a large heavy-based frying pan for stir-frying, but the food will need to be cooked in smaller batches to prevent stewing.

SEASONING THE WOK

Steel woks come with an oily film which needs to be scrubbed off with hot water and detergent before use. The wok should then be dried off and heated over high heat. When it starts to become hot, brush it with vegetable oil, remove it from the heat and wipe it dry with a paper towel (it will blacken as you season it). Repeat this step several times to season the wok. As you use the wok, the seasoned layer will build up, getting darker and darker. When washing your wok, soak off any bits that are sticking and then wash it gently in hot soapy water. Do not scrub the wok with harsh abrasives or you will strip off the seasoning. Dry the wok thoroughly over heat or it will rust.

Electric woks also need to be rinsed in hot soapy water and coated with a thin film of oil before use. Wooden or plastic utensils should be used on non-stick woks so that the surface does not become scratched.

WOK TOOLS

Wooden, metal and plastic wok sangs/charns (shovel-like spatulas) are available for stir-frying. They are excellent, as are flat spatulas, because they move the food around easily and follow the curvature of the wok.

RICE

If you don't have a rice cooker, one of the best ways to cook rice is the absorption method. You will need a large shallowish heavy-based pan with a tightly fitting lid. The shallowness spreads the rice out into a thinner layer so that it all cooks evenly rather than quicker at the bottom. Before you cook it, wash the rice thoroughly in a sieve under running water until the water runs clear. For each 200 g (6½ oz) rice, add 1¼ cups (315 ml/10 fl oz) water. Bring to the boil, cover tightly with the lid and cook on very low heat for 10 minutes. Remove from the heat and leave, still covered, for 10 minutes. When you take off the lid, the surface of the rice should be dotted with steam holes. Fluff up the rice with a fork and serve.

Absorption-method rice is cooked when dotted with steam holes on top.

TYPES OF WOK

Traditional or electric woks are suitable for stir-frying.

The oily film on a new wok has to be scrubbed off before use.

A wok will blacken as you season it and get darker as you use it.

STEPS FOR SUCCESSFUL STIR-FRYING

Heat the wok, add the oil and swirl it around to coat the side of the wok.

When the oil starts to shimmer, add the first ingredients and toss.

There is an easy set of rules to follow for stir-frying.

- The most important thing is to have everything ready before you start to stir-fry. Arrange all the ingredients in bowls in the order you are going to cook them and measure out any liquids, pastes, sauces or cornflour that you might be adding. Once you start cooking, it is hard to stop and chop something up without ruining everything.

- Cut all meat and vegetables into even-sized, smallish pieces. The smaller the pieces, the faster they will cook.

- Choose vegetables which will look colourful as well as taste good with the other ingredients.

- Heat the wok until very hot before you add the oil. When you add the oil, swirl it around to coat the side of the wok. The oil will start to shimmer when it is hot enough and will hiss when the first ingredients go in.

- Drain any marinade from the ingredients before cooking and make sure all vegetables are quite dry. If any liquid hits the hot oil first, it will spit.

Stir-fry meat in batches if necessary, to prevent it stewing.

Keep the food moving to ensure even cooking and prevent burning.

- Add the flavourings, such as ginger and garlic, first, then add the slower-cooking ingredients, followed by the faster-cooking ones. If you have too much to fit in the wok at one time, fry the meat first in batches and set it aside, otherwise it will stew. Salty liquids, such as soy sauce, should be added at the end as they may draw water out of the vegetables and make them mushy.

- Keep all the ingredients moving constantly around the wok to make sure everything cooks evenly and doesn't start to burn.

- If an ingredient looks as if it might burn, quickly add the next ingredient because this will reduce the temperature of the wok.

- If the ingredients start to look a little dry, add a splash of water.

- Serve immediately—stir-fries don't wait for anyone!

Glossary of ingredients

Stir-fries use the best of fresh produce and exotic flavours. Ingredients such as bok choy and mirin are becoming popular and are widely available. Other items may require a visit to an Asian supermarket.

BBQ CHINESE PORK (CHAR SIEW)
Pork which has been marinated in five spice powder, soy sauce, sugar and annatto and then barbecued.

BBQ DUCK PANCAKES
Round wrappers, made with wheat flour, which are traditionally eaten with Peking duck. They are sold frozen at Asian supermarkets or ask for them when you buy your barbecued duck.

BLACK BEANS
Salted black beans are available in bags from Asian stores. They should be whole and dark and must be rinsed in cold water to get rid of excess saltiness. Chop the beans for a more robust flavour.

BLACK FUNGUS
Also know as wood ear or cloud ear mushroom, it has a mushroom flavour and a chewy crunchy texture. Dried black fungus should be soaked in boiling water for 30 minutes before cooking.

BOK CHOY
Bok choy has fleshy white stems and dark green leaves. It is also available as pak choi, baby bok choy and Shanghai bok choy which has a pale green stem.

CHOY SUM
Flowering Chinese cabbage with green stems and yellow flowers. This is often confused with gai laan (Chinese broccoli) which is similar in appearance but has white flowers. They are inter-changeable in recipes.

FISH SAUCE

This is a thin salty sauce with a distinctive fishy aroma which is stronger than its flavour. It is usually used as a seasoning at the end of cooking to balance sweetness and add saltiness.

GAI LAAN

Chinese broccoli or Chinese kale has smooth round stems with dark green leaves and small white flowers. The stems are the part most commonly eaten.

HALOUMI

A mild, salty cheese from Cyprus made from milk from goats, sheep or cows. It comes in a firm block and can be cut into cubes or sliced before being fried or grilled to give it a toasted coating. Delicious in salads or with vegetable stir-fries.

HOISIN SAUCE

A thick, reddish brown sauce, made from soy beans, garlic, sugar and spices. It has a sweet, spicy flavour and is used in cooking and for dipping.

HOT BEAN PASTE

Made from fermented soy beans and chilli, this sauce can be very hot and should be used with care.

KAFFIR LIMES AND LIME LEAVES

Kaffir limes have a knobbly skin which can be grated (the juice is not used). The leaves are used whole or finely shredded to give citrus flavour and are available fresh and dried (the dried must be soaked).

KECAP MANIS

A very thick, dark, sweet soy sauce from Indonesia. It is used in cooking as a seasoning, or as an ingredient in dipping sauces.

MIRIN

This low-alcohol rice wine, made from sake, is used in Japanese dishes such as yakitori and teriyaki. The sugar content helps to glaze the food when it is cooked. Choose pure mirin as some brands are a sweet seasoning type which have corn syrup and salt added.
If mirin is not available, you can use dry sherry.

MUSHROOMS

Shiitake, oyster, shemiji, enoki are all types of mushroom used in Asian cookery and available fresh from supermarkets. Straw mushrooms, grown in straw, have globe-shaped caps and no stems. They are available in cans and have a musty flavour.

PALM SUGAR

A caramel-flavoured aromatic sugar extracted from the sap of sugar palms. It is sold in blocks or jars and comes in a variety of colours. Soft brown sugar can be used instead.

RICE WINE (SHAO HSING)

A Chinese cooking wine that has been aged, this is amber-coloured and has a flavour similar to sherry, which can be used as a substitute. Do not confuse with rice wine vinegar.

SAMBAL OELEK

Sambal oelek is a hot chilli paste made from chillies, salt and vinegar, usually with the chilli seeds left in. A spoonful of sambal oelek will add heat to any dish.

SEASONING SAUCE

A thin, salty soy bean seasoning sauce used in Asian cooking to enhance the flavour of dishes. It is also available as Golden Mountain sauce and Maggi Seasoning sauce.

SHRIMP PASTE

This very pungent flavouring is made from fermented shrimps and is sold as a paste or in a block. It has to be cooked before eating, to release its flavour. Store well wrapped in an airtight container.

SZECHWAN PEPPER

Szechwan (Sichuan) pepper is a tiny red berry not related to ordinary peppercorns. It is aromatic and is one of the ingredients in five spice powder. Remove the black seeds and dry fry it to bring out its full flavour before using it in cooking.

TAMARI

A dark, richly flavoured Japanese soy sauce made from rice rather than wheat. It can be used either as a dipping sauce or as a seasoning.

Noodles

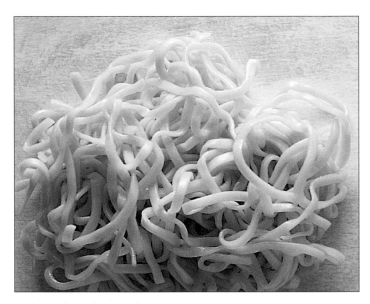

FRESH EGG NOODLES
These are made from egg and wheat flour and need to be cooked in boiling water before use. Refrigerate until ready to use.

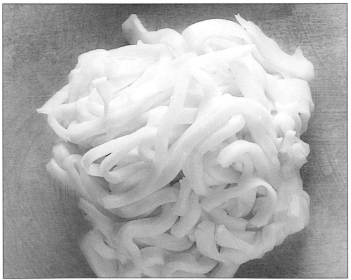

FRESH RICE NOODLES
Available thick or thin, or as a sheet or roll which can be cut to a desired width, these white rice noodles are steamed and lightly oiled before packing, and so are ready to use. They must be brought to room temperature before use, as they harden during refrigeration.

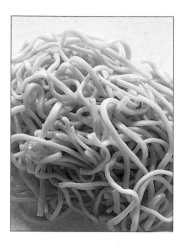

HOKKIEN NOODLES

These yellow, thick noodles are made from wheat flour and egg. They are pre-cooked and lightly oiled, so are ready to use. Refrigerate until ready to use, then break apart and add to the dish.

INSTANT NOODLES

Different brands of dried instant noodles are stocked in supermarkets. They are made from wheat flour and are very quick to prepare.

RICE STICKS (dried)

Resembling fettucine, these flat, translucent noodles are often used in stir-fries. They are sold packaged in bundles. Soak them in warm water before using.

RICE VERMICELLI (dried)

Sold packaged in blocks, these thin, translucent noodles need to be soaked in boiling water, or boiled until tender and thoroughly drained before use.

SOBA NOODLES

A Northern Japanese speciality made from buckwheat and/or wheat flour, these are eaten hot or cold. They absorb flavour well and are good with dishes which have a strongly flavoured dressing.

UDON NOODLES

White, round or flat Japanese wheat flour noodles, these are available either dried or fresh. They plump up to become slippery, fat noodles with a unique texture.

Rice

BASMATI

With long fragrant grains which remain separate when cooked, this rice is very aromatic and complements Asian flavours well. Basmati rice is grown in India on the foothills of the Himalayas and is now popular throughout the world. Traditionally used in birianies and pillaus, where saffron is added to give the dish colour and flavour.

BROWN RICE

Brown rice has not had the bran removed and is therefore valued for its nutritional properties. Cooking is a lot slower than for white rice as it takes a considerable time for the water to break through the bran layer.

JASMINE RICE

This is a long-grain, fragrant white rice used throughout Southeast Asia. It is usually steamed, or cooked using the absorption method. Jasmine rice is served as an accompaniment to all Thai meals.

LONG-GRAIN WHITE RICE

This is the rice which is chosen above all others by the Chinese – perhaps stemming from Confucius' insistence on eating the whitest rice available. It is grown in the monsoon region of Southeast Asia and is often referred to as 'water rice'. Long-grain white rice has been processed to remove the outer hull and bran, then polished until it is white and glossy.

WILD RICE

Wild rice has a nutty flavour and a high protein content. These long dark brown grains come from an aquatic grass – so wild rice is not really a rice at all, but the grain of a water grass native to the great lakes of North America. Grown originally by the Chippewa Indians and harvested by hand, it is now farmed by machine. The grains have a delicious flavour and a distinguishable chewy texture. Wild rice requires thorough washing before use. It can be bought in small packets and is expensive compared to other rices. These days it is available mixed with brown rice and sold as a wild rice blend.

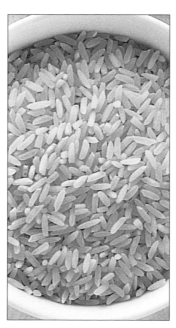

Beef and Spinach Stir-fry

PREPARATION TIME: 20 minutes
+ 2 hours marinating
TOTAL COOKING TIME: 15 minutes
SERVES 4

500 g (1 lb) rump or sirloin steak, cut into
    thin strips
¼ cup (60 ml/2 fl oz) sweet chilli sauce
2 tablespoons soy sauce
1 clove garlic, crushed
2 teaspoons grated fresh ginger
1 tablespoon sherry
oil, for cooking
2 onions, cut into wedges
500 g (1 lb) English spinach leaves, shredded

1 Combine the steak with the sweet chilli sauce, soy sauce, garlic, ginger and sherry. Cover and refrigerate for at least 2 hours, or overnight.

2 Drain the meat. Heat the wok until very hot, add 1 tablespoon of the oil and swirl it around to coat the side. Stir-fry the meat in batches over high heat until it is well browned, adding more oil when necessary. Remove from the wok and set aside.

3 Reheat the wok, add 1 tablespoon of the oil and stir-fry the onion wedges for 3–4 minutes, or until tender. Return the meat to the wok.

4 Just before serving, toss the English spinach through the beef mixture until the spinach is just wilted. Serve immediately.

Carefully slice the beef into thin strips across the grain.

Drain all the liquid from the marinated meat using a sieve.

Toss English spinach through beef mixture until spinach is wilted.

San Choy Bau

PREPARATION TIME: 25 minutes
+ 10 minutes soaking
TOTAL COOKING TIME: 8 minutes
SERVES 4

4 dried Chinese mushrooms
oil, for cooking
¼ cup (30 g/1 oz) slivered almonds, chopped
125 g (4 oz) water chestnuts, drained and
  finely chopped
1 carrot, finely chopped
4 spring onions, finely chopped
250 g (8 oz) lean pork mince
4 coriander roots, finely chopped
1 tablespoon grated fresh ginger
12 lettuce leaves, washed and dried
hoisin sauce, to serve

Sauce
1 tablespoon light soy sauce
1 tablespoon lime juice
1 teaspoon sesame oil
¼ cup (15 g/½ oz) chopped fresh coriander
2 tablespoons chopped fresh mint

1 Soak mushrooms in hot water for 10 minutes. Discard stems and chop mushrooms finely. Set aside.

2 To make the sauce, combine the soy sauce, lime juice, oil, coriander and mint. Set aside.

3 Heat the wok until very hot, add 1 tablespoon of oil and swirl it around to coat the side. Stir-fry the almonds, water chestnuts, carrot and spring onion for 1 minute, or until lightly cooked but not browned. Remove from the wok and set aside.

4 Reheat the wok and add 1 tablespoon of the oil. Stir-fry the pork mince, coriander root, ginger and mushrooms over medium-high heat for 2–3 minutes, or until the pork changes colour, but do not overcook.

5 Add the sauce and stir to combine. Return the vegetable mixture to the wok and stir-fry for 1–2 minutes, or until heated through and the mixture is well combined. Spoon the pork mixture into the lettuce leaves, sprinkle with the hoisin sauce, to taste, and fold into parcels.

Using a large sharp knife, finely chop the water chestnuts.

Discard the tough stems and finely chop the mushrooms.

Stir-fry pork mince with coriander root, ginger and mushrooms.

Spicy Sausage Stir-fry

PREPARATION TIME: 40 minutes
TOTAL COOKING TIME: 15 minutes
SERVES 4

2 tablespoons oil
500 g (1 lb) potato, cubed
500 g (1 lb) orange sweet potato, cubed
6 chorizo sausages, diagonally sliced
2 cloves garlic, thinly sliced
1 red onion, cut into wedges
200 g (6½ oz) broccoli, cut into small florets
1 red capsicum, cut into short thick strips
½ cup (125 ml/4 fl oz) tomato purée
2 tablespoons chopped fresh parsley

1 Heat the wok until very hot, add the oil and swirl it around to coat the side. Stir-fry the potato and sweet potato over medium heat until tender and golden. Remove and drain on paper towels, then place on a serving plate and cover to keep warm.

2 Add the sausage to the wok and stir-fry in batches over high heat for 3–4 minutes, or until crisp. Remove and drain on paper towels.

3 Add the garlic and onion to the wok, and stir-fry for 2 minutes, or until the onion softens. Add the broccoli and capsicum, and stir-fry for 1 minute. Return the sausage to the wok, add the tomato purée and toss to combine. Add the parsley and season with salt and freshly ground black pepper. Toss well and serve on top of the stir-fried potato.

Peel skin from the sweet potato and cut the flesh into cubes.

Cut the chorizo sausages into thick diagonal slices.

Stir-fry potato and sweet potato in hot oil until tender and golden.

Sweet Mustard Lamb Stir-fry

PREPARATION TIME: 15 minutes
TOTAL COOKING TIME: 15 minutes
SERVES 4

oil, for cooking
500 g (1 lb) lamb fillet, cut into thin strips
2 cloves garlic, crushed
250 g (8 oz) snow peas
1 onion, cut into large wedges
20 g (¾ oz) butter
¼ cup (60 g/2 oz) wholegrain mustard
1 tablespoon honey
½ cup (125 ml/4 fl oz) cream
2 tablespoons brandy, optional

1 Heat the wok until very hot, add 1 tablespoon of the oil and swirl it around to coat the side. Stir-fry the lamb strips in batches over high heat. Remove from the wok and set aside.

2 Heat 1 tablespoon of the oil in the wok and add the crushed garlic, snow peas and onion wedges. Stir-fry over medium heat for 3–4 minutes, or until the onion softens slightly. Remove from the wok and keep warm.

3 Reduce the heat and add the butter, wholegrain mustard, honey, cream and brandy to the wok. Simmer the sauce gently for 3–4 minutes. Return the meat and the snow pea mixture to the wok, and stir until the meat and vegetables are heated through and combined with the sauce.

Remove fat or sinew from lamb fillet, and cut lamb into thin strips.

Stir-fry the lamb slices in batches over high heat.

Heat the oil and add the garlic, snow peas and onion wedges.

Barbecued Pork and Broccoli Stir-fry

PREPARATION TIME: 25 minutes
TOTAL COOKING TIME: 10 minutes
SERVES 4–6

1 tablespoon oil
1 large onion, thinly sliced
2 carrots, cut into matchsticks
200 g (6½ oz) broccoli, cut into bite-sized
   florets
6 spring onions, diagonally sliced
1 tablespoon finely chopped fresh ginger
3 cloves garlic, finely chopped
400 g (13 oz) Chinese barbecued pork,
   thinly sliced
2 tablespoons soy sauce
2 tablespoons mirin
2 cups (180 g/6 oz) bean sprouts

1 Heat the wok until very hot, add the oil and swirl it around to coat the side. Stir-fry the onion over medium heat for 3–4 minutes, or until slightly softened. Add the carrot, broccoli, spring onion, ginger and garlic, and cook for 4–5 minutes, tossing constantly.

2 Increase the heat to high and add the barbecued pork. Toss constantly until the pork is well mixed with the vegetables and is heated through. Add the soy sauce and mirin, and toss until the ingredients are well coated. (The wok should be hot enough that the sauce reduces a little to form a glaze-like consistency.) Add the bean sprouts and season well with salt and pepper. Serve immediately.

Peel carrots, if necessary, and cut them into even-sized matchsticks.

Cut the pieces of Chinese barbecued pork into thin slices.

Add pork to wok and toss until it is well mixed with the vegetables.

Satay Lamb

PREPARATION TIME: 20 minutes
TOTAL COOKING TIME: 15 minutes
SERVES 4–6

oil, for cooking
500 g (1 lb) lamb fillet, thinly sliced
1 onion, chopped
2 cloves garlic, crushed
2 teaspoons grated fresh ginger
1–2 red chillies, seeded and finely chopped
1 teaspoon ground cumin
1 teaspoon ground coriander
½ cup (125 g/4 oz) crunchy peanut butter
1 tablespoon soy sauce
2 tablespoons lemon juice
½ cup (125 ml/4 fl oz) coconut cream

1 Heat the wok until very hot, add 1 tablespoon oil and swirl it around to coat the side. Stir-fry the lamb in batches over high heat until it is well browned and cooked, adding more oil when necessary. Remove the lamb from the wok and set aside.

2 Reheat the wok, add 1 tablespoon of the oil and stir-fry the onion over medium heat for 2–3 minutes, or until soft and transparent. Stir in the garlic, ginger, chilli, cumin and coriander, and cook for 1 minute.

3 Stir in the peanut butter, soy sauce, lemon juice, coconut cream and ½ cup (125 ml/4 fl oz) water. Slowly bring to the boil. Return the lamb to the wok and stir until heated through.

Stir-fry onion over medium heat until it is soft and transparent.

Add garlic, ginger, chilli, cumin and coriander to the onion.

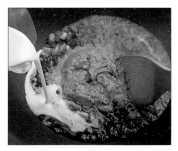

Stir in the remaining ingredients and bring to the boil.

Pork and Snake Bean Stir-fry

PREPARATION TIME: 15 minutes
TOTAL COOKING TIME: 20 minutes
SERVES 4

oil, for cooking
400 g (13 oz) pork fillet, cut into thick slices
2 onions, thinly sliced
150 g (5 oz) snake beans, diagonally sliced
3 cloves garlic, finely chopped
1 tablespoon finely chopped fresh ginger
1 red capsicum, thinly sliced
6 spring onions, diagonally sliced
2 tablespoons sweet chilli sauce

1 Heat the wok until very hot, add 2 teaspoons of the oil and swirl it around to coat the side. Stir-fry the pork in two batches over high heat for 3–4 minutes, or until it is just cooked, adding more oil when necessary. Remove all the pork from the wok.

2 Heat 1 tablespoon of the oil over medium heat and add the sliced onion. Cook for 3–4 minutes, or until the onion has softened slightly. Add the sliced snake beans and cook for 2–3 minutes. Add the garlic, ginger, capsicum and spring onion, and toss well. Increase the heat and cook for 3–4 minutes.

3 Return the pork to the wok, add the sweet chilli sauce and toss until combined. Remove from the heat and season well with salt and pepper. Serve immediately.

Top and tail snake beans, then cut them into diagonal slices.

Honey and Black Pepper Beef

PREPARATION TIME: 15 minutes
TOTAL COOKING TIME: 10 minutes
SERVES 4

oil, for cooking
500 g (1 lb) round steak, cut into thin strips
2 cloves garlic, crushed
1 onion, sliced
300 g (10 oz) sugar snap peas
2 tablespoons honey
2 teaspoons soy sauce
2 tablespoons oyster sauce
3 teaspoons cracked black pepper

1 Heat the wok until very hot, add 1 tablespoon of the oil and swirl it around to coat the side. Stir-fry the beef in batches over high heat. Remove and drain on paper towels.

2 Reheat the wok, add 1 tablespoon of the oil and stir-fry the garlic, onion and sugar snap peas until softened. Remove from the wok and set aside.

3 Add the honey, soy sauce, oyster sauce and cracked pepper to the wok. Bring to the boil, then reduce the heat and simmer for 3–4 minutes, or until the sauce thickens slightly.

4 Increase the heat, return the meat and vegetables to the wok, and toss for 2–3 minutes, or until well combined and heated through.

Swirl the oil around to coat the side of the hot wok.

Once beef is cooked, remove from wok and drain on paper towels.

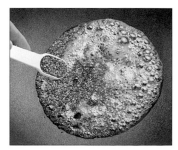

Add honey, soy and oyster sauces, and pepper and bring to the boil.

Lamb and Spinach Stir-fry

PREPARATION TIME: 20 minutes
+ 2 hours marinating
TOTAL COOKING TIME: 20 minutes
SERVES 4

2 cloves garlic, finely chopped
1 tablespoon finely chopped fresh ginger
½ teaspoon salt
1 tablespoon ground cumin
1 tablespoon ground coriander
1 teaspoon ground cinnamon
½ teaspoon ground allspice
¼ cup (60 ml/2 fl oz) oil
600 g (1¼ lb) lamb fillet, sliced diagonally
oil, for cooking
2 onions, thinly sliced
500 g (1 lb) English spinach, shredded
1 tablespoon lime juice
2 tablespoons toasted pine nuts

1 Combine the garlic, ginger, salt, spices and oil in a shallow glass or ceramic bowl. Add the sliced lamb and mix until well combined. Cover and refrigerate for at least 2 hours.

2 Heat the wok until very hot, and stir-fry the lamb in three batches over high heat for 2–3 minutes, or until the lamb is golden brown and just cooked. Remove the lamb from the wok and cover to keep warm.

3 Reheat the wok and add 1 tablespoon of the oil. Stir-fry the sliced onion over medium-high heat for 2–3 minutes, or until slightly softened. Add the spinach, cover and steam for 1–2 minutes, or until the spinach has just wilted. Return all the lamb and juices to the wok along with the lime juice and toasted pine nuts. Toss until thoroughly combined and season well with salt and pepper. Serve immediately.

Toast the pine nuts by dry-frying them in the wok.

Stir-fry the marinated lamb in batches over high heat.

Cover and steam the spinach until it has just wilted.

Coriander Beef

PREPARATION TIME: 15 minutes
+ 1–2 hours marinating
TOTAL COOKING TIME: 15 minutes
SERVES 4

500 g (1 lb) rump steak, cut into thin strips
4 cloves garlic, finely chopped
1 tablespoon finely chopped fresh ginger
½ cup (25 g/¾ oz) chopped fresh coriander
  roots, stems and leaves
¼ cup (60 ml/2 fl oz) oil
oil, extra, for cooking
2 red onions, thinly sliced
½ red capsicum, thinly sliced
½ green capsicum, thinly sliced
1 tablespoon lime juice
½ cup (25 g/¾ oz) chopped fresh coriander
  leaves, extra

1 Place the beef strips in a glass or ceramic bowl. Add the garlic, ginger, coriander and oil. Mix together well, then cover and refrigerate for 1–2 hours.

2 Heat the wok until very hot and stir-fry the meat in three batches over high heat for 2–3 minutes, or until the meat is just cooked. Remove all the meat from the wok and keep it warm.

3 Heat 1 tablespoon oil, add the onion and cook over medium-high heat for 3–4 minutes, or until slightly softened. Add the capsicum, and cook, tossing constantly, for 3–4 minutes, or until the capsicum is slightly softened.

4 Return all the meat to the wok with the lime juice and extra coriander. Toss well, then remove from the heat and season well with salt and freshly cracked black pepper. Serve immediately.

Finely chop the roots, stems and leaves of the coriander.

Stir-fry the marinated meat in batches until it is just cooked.

Add capsicum and toss constantly until it is slightly softened.

Stir-fried Beef, Leek and Snow Peas

PREPARATION TIME: 25 minutes

TOTAL COOKING TIME: 15 minutes

SERVES 4

oil, for cooking

375 g (12 oz) rump steak, cut into very thin strips

2–3 cloves garlic, finely chopped

1 stem lemon grass, white part only, finely chopped

1 leek, white part only, thinly sliced

2 celery sticks, thickly sliced

8 spring onions, diagonally sliced

150 g (5 oz) snow peas, halved

100 g (3½ oz) oyster mushrooms, halved

2 tablespoons kecap manis

2 tablespoons sweet chilli sauce

2 tablespoons lime or lemon juice

3 kaffir lime leaves, shredded

1 tablespoon fish sauce

1 Heat the wok until very hot, add 1 tablespoon of the oil and swirl it around to coat the side. Stir-fry the beef strips, garlic and lemon grass in two or three batches over high heat for 2–3 minutes, or until the beef is browned. Remove all the beef mixture from the wok.

2 Reheat the wok, add 1 tablespoon of the oil and stir-fry the leek, celery and spring onion for 2 minutes. Add the snow peas and oyster mushrooms, and stir-fry for 1–2 minutes, or until tender. Remove the vegetables from the wok and set aside.

3 Add the combined kecap manis, chilli sauce and lime or lemon juice to the wok, and bring to the boil. Return all the beef and vegetables to the wok and stir-fry for 1–2 minutes, or until the beef has just heated through and everything is well coated with the sauce. Toss the shredded kaffir lime leaves through the mixture and sprinkle with the fish sauce, to taste. Serve at once.

Finely chop the lemon grass, using only the white part.

Stir-fry the beef, garlic and lemon grass until the beef browns.

Chicken and Cashew Stir-fry

PREPARATION TIME: 30 minutes
TOTAL COOKING TIME: 20 minutes
SERVES 4–6

oil, for cooking
750 g (1½ lb) chicken thigh fillets, cut into strips
2 egg whites, lightly beaten
½ cup (60 g/2 oz) cornflour
2 onions, thinly sliced
1 red capsicum, thinly sliced
200 g (6½ oz) broccoli, cut into bite-sized pieces
2 tablespoons soy sauce
2 tablespoons sherry
1 tablespoon oyster sauce
⅓ cup (50 g/1¾ oz) roasted cashews
4 spring onions, diagonally sliced

1 Heat the wok until very hot, add 1 tablespoon of the oil and swirl it around to coat the side. Dip about a quarter of the chicken strips into the egg white and then into the cornflour. Add to the wok and stir-fry for 3–5 minutes, or until the chicken is golden brown and just cooked. Drain on paper towels and repeat with the remaining chicken, reheating the wok and adding a little more oil each time.

2 Reheat the wok, add 1 tablespoon of the oil and stir-fry the onion, capsicum and broccoli over medium heat for 4–5 minutes, or until the vegetables have softened slightly. Increase the heat to high and add the soy sauce, sherry and oyster sauce. Toss the vegetables well in the sauce and bring to the boil.

3 Return the chicken to the wok and toss over high heat for 1–2 minutes to heat the chicken and make sure it is entirely cooked through. Season well with salt and freshly cracked pepper. Toss the cashews and spring onion through the chicken mixture, and serve immediately.

Dip chicken strips into the egg white, then into the cornflour.

Stir-fry the chicken in batches until it is golden brown.

39

Honey Chicken

PREPARATION TIME: 15 minutes
TOTAL COOKING TIME: 25 minutes
SERVES 4

oil, for cooking
500 g (1 lb) chicken thigh fillets, cut into
  cubes
1 egg white, lightly beaten
⅓ cup (40 g/1¼ oz) cornflour
2 onions, thinly sliced
1 green capsicum, cubed
2 carrots, cut into batons
100 g (3½ oz) snow peas, sliced
¼ cup (90 g/3 oz) honey
2 tablespoons toasted almonds

1 Heat the wok until very hot, add 1½ tablespoons of the oil and swirl it around to coat the side. Dip half of the chicken into the egg white, then lightly dust with the cornflour. Stir-fry over high heat for 4–5 minutes, or until the chicken is golden brown and just cooked. Remove from the wok and drain on paper towels. Repeat with the remaining chicken, then remove all the chicken from the wok.

2 Reheat the wok, add 1 tablespoon of the oil and stir-fry the sliced onion over high heat for 3–4 minutes, or until slightly softened. Add the capsicum and carrot, and cook, tossing constantly, for 3–4 minutes, or until tender. Stir in the snow peas and cook for 2 minutes.

3 Increase the heat, add the honey and toss the vegetables until well coated. Return the chicken to the wok and toss until it is heated through and is well coated in the honey. Remove from the heat and season well with salt and pepper. Serve immediately, sprinkled with the almonds.

Trim excess fat from the chicken, and cut the chicken into cubes.

Dip chicken into egg white, then lightly dust with the cornflour.

Stir-fry the chicken pieces until golden brown and just cooked.

Peking-style Duck with Spring Onion and Plum Sauce

PREPARATION TIME: 15 minutes
TOTAL COOKING TIME: 15 minutes
SERVES 2–3

½ Chinese barbecued duck (about 500 g/1 lb), boned
1 tablespoon oil
12 spring onions, cut into 5 cm (2 inch) pieces
1 large carrot, cut into batons
1 tablespoon cornflour
1 tablespoon honey
1 tablespoon sherry
1 tablespoon vinegar
¼ cup (60 ml/2 fl oz) plum sauce
1 tablespoon soy sauce
12 barbecued duck pancakes, to serve

1 Remove and discard any excess fat and some of the skin from the duck. Cut the duck into bite-sized pieces. Heat the wok until very hot, add the duck pieces and cook over high heat for 3–4 minutes, or until the skin starts to become crispy. Remove from the wok.

2 Reheat wok, add oil and swirl it around to coat the side. Stir-fry spring onion and carrot over medium heat for 3–4 minutes, or until carrot has softened slightly. Combine cornflour with honey, sherry, vinegar, plum sauce and soy sauce. Increase the heat to high, return the duck to the wok and toss well. When the wok is very hot, add the sauce mixture and toss constantly for 2–3 minutes to coat the duck and vegetables. The sauce will begin to caramelise and reduce to form a glaze.

3 Remove the wok from the heat. Serve the stir-fried duck mixture with the pancakes, which have been steamed for 3–4 minutes or warmed in the microwave. To serve, place a small portion of the duck in the middle of a pancake, fold in the edges and roll it up.

Ask to have the barbecued duck boned when you buy it.

Add sauce and toss until sauce caramelises and reduces.

Stir-fried Chicken, Lemon and Capers

PREPARATION TIME: 15 minutes
TOTAL COOKING TIME: 15 minutes
SERVES 4

olive oil, for cooking
1 red onion, cut into thin wedges
25 g (¾ oz) butter
800 g (1 lb 10 oz) chicken breast fillets, cut
  into bite-sized pieces
rind of 1 lemon, cut into thin strips
2 tablespoons baby capers, rinsed well and
  drained
⅓ cup (80 ml/2¾ fl oz) lemon juice
¼ cup (15 g/½ oz) shredded fresh basil

1 Heat the wok until very hot, add 2 teaspoons of the oil and swirl it around to coat the side. Add the red onion wedges and stir-fry until softened and golden. Remove from the wok and set aside.

2 Reheat the wok, add 2 teaspoons of the oil and half the butter, and stir-fry the chicken in two batches until it is browned, adding more oil and butter between batches. Return all the chicken to the wok with the onion.

3 Stir in the lemon rind, capers and lemon juice. Toss well and cook until warmed through. Add the shredded basil and season with salt and black pepper. Delicious served with creamy mashed potato.

Peel the red onion, cut it in half and cut it into thin wedges.

Use a zester to remove thin strips of rind from the lemon.

Stir-fry the onion wedges until they are soft and golden.

Chicken with Beans and Asparagus

PREPARATION TIME: 25 minutes
+ 15 minutes marinating
TOTAL COOKING TIME: 15 minutes
SERVES 4

1 stem lemon grass, white part only, chopped
5 cm (2 inch) piece fresh ginger, peeled and
  chopped
2–3 small red chillies, seeded and chopped
1 teaspoon grated kaffir lime or lime rind
2–3 cloves garlic, chopped
½ teaspoon ground black pepper
2 tablespoons oil
375 g (12 oz) chicken breast fillets, cut into
  thin strips
250 g (8 oz) green beans, cut into short pieces
1 celery stick, cut into short slices
185 g (6 oz) snow peas, halved
200 g (6½ oz) asparagus, cut into short
  pieces
270 ml (9 fl oz) can coconut cream
2 tablespoons sweet chilli sauce
20 small fresh basil leaves

1 Place the lemon grass, ginger, chilli, lime rind, garlic, black pepper and oil in a food processor or blender, and process until the mixture forms a rough paste. Combine the paste and chicken strips in a glass or ceramic bowl, cover and refrigerate for at least 15 minutes.

2 Briefly blanch the beans, celery, snow peas and asparagus in a pan of boiling water. Drain and plunge into iced water. Drain again.

3 Heat the wok until very hot and stir-fry the chicken mixture in batches over high heat for 3–4 minutes, or until the chicken is cooked through. Stir constantly so the paste doesn't burn. Add the vegetables, coconut cream, sweet chilli sauce, to taste, and basil leaves. Stir-fry until heated through. Serve with rice or noodles.

Grating rind is easier if you fit a piece of baking paper over grater.

Process the herbs and oil to a thick paste.

47

Duck and Orange Stir-fry

PREPARATION TIME: 25 minutes
TOTAL COOKING TIME: 15 minutes
SERVES 4

1 Chinese barbecued duck (about 1 kg/2 lb),
  boned
1 tablespoon oil
1 onion, sliced
2 cloves garlic, crushed
2 teaspoons grated fresh ginger
1 tablespoon orange rind
⅔ cup (170 ml/5½ fl oz) orange juice
¼ cup (60 ml/2 fl oz) chicken stock
2 teaspoons soft brown sugar
2 teaspoons cornflour
1.5 kg (3 lb) baby bok choy, leaves separated
1 orange, segmented

1 Cut the duck meat into pieces. Reserve and thinly slice some crispy skin for garnish. Heat the wok until very hot, add the oil and swirl it around to coat the side. Stir-fry the onion for 3 minutes, or until tender. Stir in the garlic and ginger for 1–2 minutes. Pour in the combined orange rind, juice, stock and sugar. Bring to the boil.

2 Mix the cornflour with a little water to form a paste. Pour into the wok, stirring until the mixture boils and thickens. Place the duck pieces in the sauce and simmer for 1–2 minutes, or until heated through. Remove from the wok and keep warm.

3 Place the bok choy in the wok with 2 tablespoons water. Cover and steam until just wilted. Arrange on a serving plate, spoon the duck mixture over the top and garnish with the orange segments and the crispy duck skin.

Cut downwards to remove the rind and pith from the orange.

Segment orange by slicing between membrane and flesh.

Ask to have the barbecued duck boned when you buy it.

Stir-fried Chicken and Pasta

PREPARATION TIME: 20 minutes

TOTAL COOKING TIME: 15 minutes

SERVES 4–6

270 g (9 oz) jar sun-dried tomatoes in oil
500 g (1 lb) chicken breast fillets, cut into
   thin strips
2 cloves garlic, crushed
½ cup (125 ml/4 fl oz) cream
2 tablespoons shredded fresh basil
400 g (13 oz) penne pasta, cooked
2 tablespoons pine nuts, toasted

1 Drain the sun-dried tomatoes, reserving the oil. Thinly slice the sun-dried tomatoes.

2 Heat the wok until very hot, add 1 tablespoon of the reserved oil and swirl it around to coat the side. Stir-fry the chicken strips in batches, adding more oil when necessary.

3 Return all the chicken strips to the wok and add the garlic, sun-dried tomatoes and cream. Simmer gently for 4–5 minutes.

4 Stir in the basil and pasta, and heat through. Season well. Serve topped with the toasted pine nuts.

Toast the pine nuts by dry-frying them in the wok.

Drain sun-dried tomatoes and thinly slice them.

Return chicken to wok with garlic, sun-dried tomatoes and cream.

Stir-fried Sesame Chicken and Leek

PREPARATION TIME: 15 minutes
TOTAL COOKING TIME: 16 minutes
SERVES 4–6

2 tablespoons sesame seeds
1 tablespoon oil
2 teaspoons sesame oil
800 g (1 lb 10 oz) chicken tenderloins, cut
  diagonally into strips
1 leek, white part only, julienned
2 cloves garlic, crushed
2 tablespoons soy sauce
1 tablespoon mirin
1 teaspoon sugar

1 Heat the wok until very hot, add the sesame seeds and dry-fry over high heat until they are golden. Remove the seeds from the wok.

2 Reheat the wok, add the oils and swirl them around to coat the side. Stir-fry the chicken strips in three batches over high heat, tossing constantly until just cooked. Reheat the wok before each addition. Return all the chicken to the wok.

3 Add the julienned leek and the garlic and cook for 1–2 minutes, or until the leek is soft and golden. Check that the chicken is cooked through; if it is not cooked, reduce the heat and cook, covered, for 2 minutes, or until it is completely cooked.

4 Add the soy sauce, mirin, sugar and toasted sesame seeds to the wok, and toss well to combine. Season with salt and black pepper, and serve immediately. Delicious with pasta.

Cut the chicken tenderloins into thin diagonal strips.

Cut the white part of the leek into julienne strips.

Dry-fry the sesame seeds over high heat, stirring, until golden.

Warm Prawn and Scallop Salad

PREPARATION TIME: 30 minutes
+ 10 minutes marinating
TOTAL COOKING TIME: 15 minutes
SERVES 4

2 teaspoons five-spice powder
1–2 small red chillies, seeded and finely
  chopped
2–3 cloves garlic, crushed
2 tablespoons oil
2 teaspoons sesame oil
24 raw prawns, peeled and deveined, tails
  intact
20 scallops, cleaned
200 g (6½ oz) fresh asparagus, cut into pieces
150 g (5 oz) snow peas
125 g (4 oz) rocket leaves
2 tablespoons light soy sauce
2 tablespoons lemon juice
1 tablespoon mirin
1 tablespoon oil
1 tablespoon honey
6 spring onions, chopped
⅓ cup (20 g/¾ oz) chopped coriander leaves
1 tablespoon sesame seeds, lightly toasted

1 Combine the five-spice powder, chilli, garlic and oils in a large glass or ceramic bowl. Add the prawns and scallops and toss to coat. Cover and refrigerate for at least 10 minutes.

2 Blanch the asparagus and snow peas briefly in a pan of boiling water. Drain and plunge into a bowl of iced water, then drain again. Tear the rocket leaves if they are too big. Arrange the asparagus, snow peas and rocket on four serving plates.

3 Put the soy sauce, lemon juice, mirin, oil and honey in a small bowl. Stir to combine.

4 Heat the wok until very hot and stir-fry the prawns, scallops and spring onion over high heat in three or four batches for 3–4 minutes, or until cooked through. Remove from the wok and set aside.

5 Add the sauce and coriander to the wok, and bring to the boil. Cook over high heat for 1–2 minutes. Return the seafood mixture to the wok and toss well. Divide the mixture among the serving plates and sprinkle with the sesame seeds.

Peel prawns, leaving tails intact, and pull out the dark veins.

Slice off any vein, membrane or hard white muscle from scallops.

Marinated Chilli Squid

PREPARATION TIME: 10 minutes
+ 2–3 hours marinating
TOTAL COOKING TIME: 15 minutes
SERVES 4

500 g (1 lb) squid tubes
1 tablespoon finely chopped fresh ginger
2–3 teaspoons finely chopped red chilli
3 cloves garlic, finely chopped
¼ cup (60 ml/2 fl oz) oil
2 onions, thinly sliced
500 g (1 lb) baby bok choy, roughly
  chopped

1 Wash the squid well and dry with paper towels. Cut into 1 cm (½ inch) rings and place in a shallow glass or ceramic bowl. Combine the ginger, chilli, garlic and oil. Pour the mixture over the squid and toss well. Cover and refrigerate for 2–3 hours.

2 Heat the wok until very hot and stir-fry the squid rings over high heat in three batches for 1–2 minutes, reserving the marinade. Remove from the wok as soon as the squid turns white. Do not overcook or the squid will be rubbery. Remove all the squid from the wok and set aside.

3 Pour the reserved marinade into the wok and bring to the boil. Add the onion and cook over medium heat for 3–4 minutes, or until it is slightly softened. Add the bok choy and steam, covered, for 2 minutes, or until it has wilted slightly. Return the squid to the wok and toss until well combined. Season well. Remove from the wok and serve immediately.

Wash the squid well and pat dry with paper towels.

Using a sharp knife, slice the washed squid tubes into rings.

Remove squid from wok as soon as it turns white, or it will be tough.

Swordfish with Bok Choy

PREPARATION TIME: 20 minutes
TOTAL COOKING TIME: 10 minutes
SERVES 4

500 g (1 lb) swordfish steak, cut into
  bite-sized pieces
2 tablespoons freshly cracked black pepper
oil, for cooking
3 cloves garlic, thinly sliced
1 onion, sliced
1 kg (2 lb) baby bok choy, leaves separated
100 g (3½ oz) shiitake mushrooms, sliced
2 tablespoons hoisin sauce
2 tablespoons rice wine
1 tablespoon oyster sauce
1 tablespoon soy sauce
1 tablespoon toasted sesame seeds
1 teaspoon sesame oil

1 Dip the swordfish in cracked black pepper until coated, then shake off any excess.

2 Heat the wok until very hot, add 2 tablespoons of the oil and swirl it around to coat the side. Stir-fry the swordfish in batches over high heat until tender. Do not overcook or the fish will break up. Remove; keep warm.

3 Reheat the wok, add 1 tablespoon of the oil and stir-fry the garlic until crisp and golden. Add the onion and stir-fry until golden. Add the bok choy and mushrooms and cook until the leaves wilt. Combine the hoisin sauce, rice wine, oyster sauce and soy sauce in a jug. Pour into the wok and heat.

4 Return the swordfish to the wok and toss. Serve sprinkled with sesame seeds and drizzled with the oil.

Use a sharp knife to cut swordfish steak into bite-sized pieces.

Wipe mushrooms with a damp paper towel, then cut into slices.

Dip pieces of swordfish in black pepper and shake off any excess.

Szechwan Prawns with Snow Peas

PREPARATION TIME: 30 minutes
+ 20 minutes marinating
TOTAL COOKING TIME: 20 minutes
SERVES 4

2 teaspoons Szechwan pepper
750 g (1½ lb) raw prawns, peeled and
   deveined, tails intact
2 tablespoons grated fresh ginger
3 cloves garlic, finely chopped
2 tablespoons Chinese rice wine or dry
   sherry
oil, for cooking
2 eggs, lightly beaten
½ red capsicum, cut into strips
½ green capsicum, cut into strips
4 spring onions, cut into pieces
100 g (3½ oz) snow peas
½ teaspoon salt
75 g (2½ oz) roasted unsalted peanuts,
   roughly chopped
50 g (1¾ oz) snow pea sprouts

1 Heat the wok until very hot and dry-fry Szechwan pepper until it is fragrant. Remove from wok and crush with a mortar and pestle or in a spice mill.

2 Combine the prawns with the Szechwan pepper, ginger, garlic and wine in a glass or ceramic dish. Cover and refrigerate for 20 minutes.

3 Heat the wok until very hot, add 1½ tablespoons of the oil and swirl it around to coat the side. Dip three or four prawns in the beaten eggs, then stir-fry for about 1 minute, or until the prawns just change colour and are cooked. Remove from the wok. Repeat with the remaining prawns, reheating the wok to very hot for each batch and adding a little oil when needed. Remove the prawns from the wok.

4 Add the capsicum, spring onion, snow peas and salt to the wok. Stir-fry for 2 minutes, or until the vegetables are just crisp and tender.

5 Return the prawns to the wok along with the peanuts, and toss gently to combine. Serve immediately on a bed of snow pea sprouts.

Peel prawns, leaving tails intact, and pull out the dark veins.

Dry-fry the Szechwan pepper in a hot wok until it is fragrant.

Crush the fried Szechwan pepper with a mortar and pestle.

Warm Smoked Salmon, Cannellini Bean and Tomato Salad

PREPARATION TIME: 20 minutes

TOTAL COOKING TIME: 15 minutes

SERVES 4

olive oil, for cooking
6 slices white bread, cubed
3 cloves garlic, crushed
6 spring onions, sliced
300 g (10 oz) smoked salmon, cut into thin strips
300 g (10 oz) can cannellini beans, rinsed
4 Roma tomatoes, chopped
175 g (6 oz) iceberg lettuce, shredded
2 tablespoons chopped fresh dill
2 tablespoons lemon juice
2 tablespoons olive oil, extra

1 Heat the wok until very hot, add ⅓ cup (80 ml/ 2¾ fl oz) oil and swirl it around to coat the side. Stir-fry the bread over high heat until crisp and golden. Remove from the wok and drain on paper towels.

2 Reheat the wok, add 1 tablespoon of the oil and stir-fry the garlic and half the spring onion for 2 minutes. Remove from the wok.

3 Reheat the wok and stir-fry the salmon until it is slightly crisp. Add the cannellini beans and tomato, and cook for 2–3 minutes, or until heated through. Remove from the heat and quickly stir in the lettuce, dill, and the spring onion and garlic mixture.

4 Whisk the lemon juice and extra olive oil, and pour it over the salad. Add the croutons and toss. Garnish with the remaining spring onion.

Make croutons by stir-frying bread cubes until crisp and golden.

Salt-and-pepper Squid

PREPARATION TIME: 40 minutes
+ 20 minutes marinating
TOTAL COOKING TIME: 10 minutes
SERVES 4

500 g (1 lb) squid tubes
⅓ cup (80 ml/2¾ fl oz) oil
4 cloves garlic, finely chopped
½ teaspoon sugar
2 teaspoons sea salt
1 teaspoon finely ground black pepper
150 g (5 oz) baby English spinach leaves
100 g (3½ oz) cherry tomatoes, quartered
2 tablespoons lime juice
lime quarters, to garnish

1 Cut the squid tubes in half length-ways and open them out. Wash under cold water and pat dry with paper towels. Lay the tubes on a chopping board with the inside facing upwards. Honeycomb the squid by scoring along the length of each piece very finely, then diagonally across the width to create a fine diamond pattern. Cut the squid into pieces about 5 x 3 cm (2 x 1¼ inches). Combine the squid, oil, garlic, sugar and half the salt and pepper, cover and refrigerate for 20 minutes.

2 Arrange the spinach leaves and tomatoes on a large serving platter.

3 Heat the wok until it is very hot and stir-fry the squid over high heat in three or four batches, tossing constantly, for 1–2 minutes, or until the squid just turns white and curls. Remove each batch from the wok and reheat the wok in between batches.

4 Return all the squid pieces to the wok along with the lime juice and the remaining salt and pepper. Stir briefly until heated through. Arrange on top of the spinach and garnish with the lime wedges. Serve immediately.

Cut the squid tubes in half lengthways, and open them out.

Score along length, then diago-nally to create a diamond pattern.

Fold honeycombed squid tubes over and cut them into pieces.

Seafood Stir-fry

PREPARATION TIME: 20 minutes
TOTAL COOKING TIME: 15 minutes
SERVES 4–6

200 g (6½ oz) squid tubes
olive oil, for cooking
350 g (12 oz) raw prawns, peeled and
  deveined, tails intact
250 g (8 oz) firm white fish fillets, cut into
  strips
250 g (8 oz) scallops, cleaned
2 onions, thinly sliced
3 cloves garlic, finely chopped
2 tablespoons finely grated fresh ginger
1 green capsicum, thinly sliced
5 spring onions, diagonally sliced
2 tablespoons mirin
½ teaspoon salt

1 Wash and dry the squid tubes and slice into rings. Heat the wok until very hot, add 2 teaspoons of oil and swirl it around to coat the side. Stir-fry the prawns and squid rings in batches over high heat until they have just changed colour, then remove from the wok.

2 Reheat the wok, add 2 teaspoons of the oil and stir-fry the fish strips and scallops until just cooked. Do not overcook the seafood or it will break up. Remove from the wok.

3 Reheat the wok, add 1 tablespoon of the oil and stir-fry the sliced onion over medium-high heat for about 3–4 minutes, or until it has just softened. Add the garlic, ginger, capsicum and spring onion. Increase the heat to high and toss constantly for 3–4 minutes.

4 Add the mirin and salt to the wok along with some freshly cracked pepper, and toss until well combined. Return all of the seafood to the wok and toss until well combined and heated through.

Peel prawns, leaving tails intact, and pull out the dark veins.

Wash and dry the squid tubes, and slice them into rings.

Stir-fry prawns and squid rings until they have changed colour.

67

Marinated Tofu with Vegetables

PREPARATION TIME: 20 minutes
+ 2 hours marinating
TOTAL COOKING TIME: 20 minutes
SERVES 4

500 g (1 lb) firm tofu, cut into 2 cm (¾ inch) cubes
⅓ cup (80 ml/2¾ fl oz) shoyu (Japanese soy sauce)
¼ cup (60 ml/2 fl oz) mirin
3 cloves garlic, finely chopped
2 tablespoons finely chopped fresh ginger
oil, for cooking
1 onion, thinly sliced
2 carrots, cut into batons
1 red capsicum, thinly sliced
150 g (5 oz) snow peas, thinly sliced

1 Combine the tofu with the soy sauce, mirin, garlic and ginger in a glass or ceramic bowl. Cover and refrigerate for 2 hours.

2 Heat the wok until very hot, add 1 tablespoon of the oil and swirl it around to coat the side. Drain the tofu, reserving the marinade. Stir-fry the tofu in three batches over high heat until it is golden brown. Heat 1 tablespoon of the oil between batches. Remove all the tofu from the wok and drain on paper towels.

3 Reheat the wok, add 1 tablespoon of the oil and stir-fry the onion, carrot and capsicum over medium-high heat for 3–4 minutes, or until the vegetables are tender. Add the snow peas and cook for 3 minutes.

4 Increase the heat to high and add the reserved marinade, tossing the vegetables in the marinade until they are thoroughly coated and the sauce boils. Return the tofu to the wok and toss until the mixture is well combined and the tofu is heated through. Season well with salt and pepper, and serve immediately.

Drain the firm tofu, and cut into bite-sized cubes.

Combine the tofu, soy sauce, mirin, garlic and ginger in a bowl.

Combination Vegetables

PREPARATION TIME: 25 minutes
TOTAL COOKING TIME: 15 minutes
SERVES 4

1 tablespoon oil
2 onions, cut into thin wedges
3 cloves garlic, finely chopped
1 tablespoon finely chopped fresh ginger
1 red capsicum, cut into thin strips
200 g (6½ oz) broccoli, cut into bite-sized
  pieces
100 g (3½ oz) baby corn, halved lengthways
100 g (3½ oz) snow peas, sliced
1 tablespoon soy sauce
1 tablespoon hoisin sauce
2 teaspoons sugar
6 spring onions, diagonally sliced into long
  strips

1 Heat the wok until very hot, add the oil and swirl it around to coat the side. Stir-fry the onion over high heat for 3–4 minutes, or until slightly softened. Add the garlic, ginger and vegetables, and toss until well combined. Stir-fry for 2–3 minutes. Add 1 tablespoon of water, cover and cook for 1–2 minutes.

2 Increase the heat to high and stir in the soy sauce, hoisin sauce, sugar and spring onion, tossing constantly until well combined with and coating all the vegetables. Season well with salt and pepper before serving.

Peel the onions and then cut them into thin wedges.

Peel a piece of ginger and chop it finely to make up 1 tablespoon.

Slice the spring onions diagonally into long strips.

71

Stir-fried Asian Greens and Mushrooms

PREPARATION TIME: 20 minutes
TOTAL COOKING TIME: 5 minutes
SERVES 4

20 stems Chinese broccoli
4 baby bok choy
100 g (3½ oz) shimeji or enoki mushrooms
100 g (3½ oz) shiitake mushrooms
1 tablespoon soy sauce
2 teaspoons crushed palm sugar
1 tablespoon oil
4 spring onions, cut into short pieces
5 cm (2 inch) piece fresh ginger, cut into thin strips
1–2 small red chillies, seeded and finely chopped
2–3 cloves garlic, crushed
125 g (4 oz) snow peas, halved
1–2 teaspoons seasoning sauce

1 Remove any tough outer leaves from the Chinese broccoli and bok choy. Cut into 4 cm (1½ inch) pieces across the leaves, including the stems. Wash thoroughly, then drain and dry thoroughly. Wipe the mushrooms with a paper towel and trim the ends. Slice the shiitake mushrooms thickly.

2 Combine the soy sauce and palm sugar with ¼ cup (60 ml/2 fl oz) water. Set aside.

3 Heat the wok until very hot, add the oil and swirl it around to coat the side. Stir-fry the spring onion, ginger, chilli and garlic over low heat for 30 seconds, without browning. Increase the heat to high and add the Chinese broccoli, bok choy and snow peas. Stir-fry for 1–2 minutes, or until the vegetables are wilted.

4 Add the prepared mushrooms and soy sauce mixture. Stir-fry over high heat for 1–2 minutes, or until the mushrooms and sauce are heated through. Sprinkle with the seasoning sauce, to taste, and serve immediately.

You will need to gently separate the shimeji mushrooms.

Trim the shiitake mushrooms and cut them into thick slices.

Peel the piece of ginger and cut it into thin strips.

Spring Vegetables with Herbed Butter

PREPARATION TIME: 20 minutes
TOTAL COOKING TIME: 10 minutes
Serves 6 as an accompaniment

2 tablespoons light olive oil
200 g (6½ oz) asparagus, cut into short
    lengths
115 g (4 oz) baby corn, halved lengthways
250 g (8 oz) snow peas
250 g (8 oz) green beans, halved
300 g (10 oz) baby carrots, halved lengthways
2 cloves garlic, crushed
50 g (1¾ oz) unsalted butter
¼ cup (15 g/½ oz) finely chopped fresh
    parsley
¼ cup (15 g/½ oz) finely chopped fresh chives
¼ cup (15 g/½ oz) shredded fresh basil

1 Heat the wok until very hot, add the oil and swirl it around to coat the side. Stir-fry all the vegetables over high heat for 5 minutes. Cover and cook over low heat for 2 minutes, or until tender.

2 Add the crushed garlic, butter and all the fresh herbs, and toss until the butter has melted and the herbs have wilted slightly. Season well with salt and pepper and serve immediately.

Finely chop the fresh parsley, using a large sharp knife.

Stir-fry asparagus, snow peas, corn, beans and carrot over high heat.

Add the garlic, butter and herbs to the tender vegetables.

Mixed Wild Mushroom Stir-fry

PREPARATION TIME: 30 minutes
TOTAL COOKING TIME: 5 minutes
SERVE 4

20 g (¾ oz) butter
1 tablespoon oil
2 cloves garlic, crushed
1 teaspoon ground cumin
1 teaspoon ground coriander
¼ teaspoon sweet paprika
750 g (1½ lb) mixed mushrooms, cleaned
   and trimmed
2 tablespoons dry sherry
4 spring onions, sliced
¼ cup (15 g/½ oz) shredded fresh basil
2 tablespoons chopped fresh flat-leaf
   parsley

1 Heat the wok until very hot, add the butter and oil and swirl it around the side. Stir-fry the garlic, cumin, coriander and paprika for 1–2 minutes, or until fragrant. Add the mushrooms and stir-fry for 2 minutes, tossing well.

2 Add the sherry and bring to the boil. Cover and cook for 30 seconds. Toss the spring onion and herbs through the mushroom mixture.

Clean and trim the mushrooms, cutting any larger ones in half.

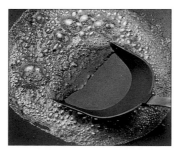

Stir-fry garlic, cumin, coriander and paprika until fragrant.

Add sherry and enoki mushrooms, cover and cook for 2 minutes.

Chilli Tempeh

PREPARATION TIME: 15 minutes
TOTAL COOKING TIME: 10 minutes
SERVES 4

250 g (8 oz) tempeh
oil, for cooking
1 onion, cut into thin slices
155 g (5 oz) asparagus, cut into short
  lengths
1 large carrot, cut into thick matchsticks
125 g (4 oz) snow peas, cut into pieces
425 g (14 oz) can baby corn, drained
2 tablespoons sweet chilli sauce
2 tablespoons kecap manis
2 tablespoons dry sherry

1 Drain the tempeh, pat dry with paper towels and cut into small pieces.

2 Heat the wok until very hot, add 2 tablespoons of the oil and swirl it around to coat the side. Stir-fry the tempeh in batches until crisp. Remove from the wok and set aside.

3 Reheat the wok, add a little more oil if necessary and stir-fry the onion for 1 minute. Add the asparagus, carrot and snow peas, and stir-fry for 2–3 minutes, or until the vegetables are just tender.

4 Return the fried tempeh to the wok and add the baby corn, sweet chilli sauce, kecap manis and sherry. Bring to the boil, simmer for 2 minutes. Toss until combined and heated, then serve.

Peel carrot, cut into short lengths, then into thick matchsticks.

Drain tempeh, dry on paper towels and cut into small pieces.

Stir-fry the pieces of tempeh in the hot oil until they are crisp.

All our recipes are thoroughly tested in a specially developed test kitchen. Standard metric measuring cups and spoons are used in the development of our recipes. All cup and spoon measurements are level. We have used 60 g (2¼ oz/Grade 3) eggs in all recipes. Sizes of cans vary from manufacturer to manufacturer and between countries – use the can size closest to the one suggested in the recipe.

CONVERSION GUIDE

1 cup = 250 ml (9 fl oz)

1 teaspoon = 5 ml

1 Australian tablespoon = 20 ml (4 teaspoons)

1 UK/US tablespoon = 15 ml (3 teaspoons)

Where temperature ranges are indicated, the lower figure applies to gas ovens, the higher to electric ovens. This allows for the fact that the flame in gas ovens generates a drier heat, which effectively cooks food faster than the moister heat of an electric oven, even if the temperature setting is the same.

DRY MEASURES	LIQUID MEASURES	LINEAR MEASURES
30 g = 1 oz	30 ml = 1 fl oz	6 mm = ¼ inch
250 g = 9 oz	125 ml = 4 fl oz	1 cm = ½ inch
500 g = 1 lb 2 oz	250 ml = 9 fl oz	2.5 cm = 1 inch

	°C	°F	GAS MARK
Very slow	120	250	½
Slow	150	300	2
Mod slow	160	325	3
Moderate	180	350	4
Mod hot	190(g)–210(e)	375–425	5
Hot	200(g)–240(e)	400–475	6
Very hot	230(g)–260(e)	450–525	8

CUP CONVERSIONS – DRY INGREDIENTS

1 cup almonds, slivered whole = 125 g (4½ oz)

1 cup cheese, lightly packed processed cheddar = 155 g (5½oz)

1 cup wheat flour = 125 g (4½ oz)

1 cup wholemeal flour = 140 g (5 oz)

1 cup minced (ground) meat = 250 g (9 oz)

1 cup pasta shapes = 125 g (4½ oz)

1 cup raisins = 170 g (6 oz)

1 cup rice, short grain, raw = 200 g (7 oz)

1 cup sesame seeds = 160 g (6 oz)

1 cup split peas = 250 g (9 oz)

(g) = gas (e) = electric

Note: For fan-forced ovens, check your appliance manual, but as a general rule, set the oven temperature to 20°C lower than the temperature indicated in the recipe.

INTERNATIONAL GLOSSARY

capsicum	sweet bell pepper	cornflour	cornstarch
chick pea	garbanzo bean	eggplant	aubergine
chilli	chile, chili pepper	spring onion	scallion
		zucchini	courgette

First published in 2008 by Murdoch Books Pty Limited,
Erico House, 6th Floor North, 93-99 Upper Richmond Road, Putney, London SW15 2TG.

This edition published 2008 for Index Books Ltd

ISBN 978 1 74196 1812

Printed by Sing Cheong Printing Co. Ltd. Printed in China.